THE POWER *of a* FRIEND

The
MESSAGE

THE READING BIBLE

WORDS TO SPEAK AND PRAY
FROM *The Message*

THE POWER *of a* FRIEND

EUGENE H. PETERSON

Bringing Truth to Life

COLORADO SPRINGS, COLORADO

The Message Editorial Team: Terry Behimer, Stephen Board, Darla Hightower, Pat Miller, Glynese Northam
The Power of a Friend Creative Team: Sarah Snelling, Mindy Mills, Ramona Richards, Darla Hightower, Laura Spray, Pat Miller

Published in association with the literary agency of Alive Communications, Inc., 7680 Goddard St., Suite 200, Colorado Springs, CO 80920.

1 2 3 4 5 6 7 8 9 10 11 12 13 14 15 16 17 / 10 09 08 07 06 05

Printed in Canada

TABLE *of* CONTENTS

Kalmia latifolia
Die breitblättrige Kalmie

The house was packed with praying friends.

—ACTS 12:12

EXPERIENCE THE POWER
of a FRIEND

We live in a time when most people live far away from their families of origin. Our friendships become the connecting places in our lives.

> *Don't leave your friends or your parents' friends*
> *and run home to your family when things get rough;*
> *Better a nearby friend*
> *than a distant family.*
> *(Proverbs 27:10)*

The Power of a Friend has been significant since the time of Solomon and before. In fact, the Bible is full of stories about friendship. David and Jonathan. Ruth and Naomi. Paul and Barnabas. Jesus and John. Friendship is powerful and it is a big part of God's story.

We have organized this book to be a tribute to the Power of a Friend. It starts with a section on loving your friends — the foundation. As 1 Corinthians 13:7 teaches us, love

> *Puts up with anything,*
> *Trusts God always,*
> *Always looks for the best,*
> *Never looks back,*
> *But keeps going to the end.*

As a basic description of friendship, it doesn't get much better than this.

We move on to stories of friends. One of the great ways that Jesus chose to teach people was through the relaying of stories. Some of our greatest examples of true friendship come from these verses. The story of Ruth begins with one of these unforgettable truths:

> *But Ruth said, "Don't force me to leave you; don't make me go home. Where you go, I go; and where you live, I'll live. Your people are my people, your God is my god; where you die, I'll die, and that's where I'll be buried, so help me God — not even death itself is going to come between us!" (Ruth 1:16-17)*

Ruth's declaration becomes a great example of the depth of God-ordained friendship.

And what would a friendship be without advice? While we live in a culture full of ideas about how to live, these timeless words of wisdom can have a great impact. Instead of using the latest trendy philosophy to encourage a friend, we can tell her: "We're the best of friends, and I pray for good fortune in everything you do, and for your good health — that your everyday affairs prosper, as well as your soul!" (3 John 1:2).

We continue with one of the most important kinds of friendship — husbands and wives. Often, we focus on the more intimate aspects of marriage, but it is the day-to-day friendship that is the true foundation of marriage. Ever practical, Ecclesiastes 4:11 tells us, "Two in a bed warm each other. Alone, you shiver all night." Even verses in Song of Solomon detail the friendship basis of marriage and highlight the importance of lifelong companionship.

The most important relationship in life is friendship with God. We learn from our early experiences with faith that we are blessed to have a "personal relationship" with God. But, what exactly is a personal relationship? Psalm 34:15 tells us that "God keeps an eye on his friends, his ears pick up every moan and groan." The verses in this group go on to cover both God's friendship with us and ours with him.

We then move back to more instructional verses with a section on how to treat people. As Christ followers who struggle to be changed "from the inside out" (Romans 12:2), these reminders can be very helpful. For example, Luke 6:28-31 tells us

> *"When someone gives you a hard time, respond with the energies of prayer for that person. If someone slaps you in the face, stand there and take it. If someone grabs your shirt, giftwrap your best coat and make a present of it. If someone takes unfair advantage of you, use the occasion to practice the servant life. No more tit-for-tat stuff. Live generously. Here is a simple rule of thumb for behavior: Ask yourself what you want people to do for you; then grab the initiative and do it for them!"*

Imagine the change we would see if we truly took these words to heart in all of our friendships.

Finally, we conclude with Jesus' friendships. Jesus' life on earth gives us many examples of what true friendship looks like. A great example of this true friendship is told in the story of Jesus washing the disciples' feet:

> *"So he got up from the supper table, set aside his robe, and put on an apron. Then he poured water into a basin and began to wash the feet of the disciples, drying them with his apron." (John 13:4-5)*

The power of a friend is to be Jesus to the people around us, to be examples of his love and to embody his Spirit.

We hope these verses and their stories of friendship will bless you and teach you. We hope that you will read them, pray them, and live them out in your own life.

— THE MESSAGE *Team*

And these God-chosen lives all around—

what splendid friends they make!

—P<small>SALM</small> 16:3

Loving Your Friends

1 Peter 4:8

> Most of all, love each other as if your life depended on it.
> Love makes up for practically anything.

John 15:12-15

> "This is my command: Love one another the way I loved
> you. This is the very best way to love. Put your life on the
> line for your friends. You are my friends when you do the
> things I command you. I'm no longer calling you servants
> because servants don't understand what their master is
> thinking and planning. No, I've named you friends because
> I've let you in on everything I've heard from the Father."

Proverbs 27: 9-10

> Just as lotions and fragrance give sensual delight,
>> a sweet friendship refreshes the soul.
>
> Don't leave your friends or your parents' friends
>> and run home to your family when things get rough;
> Better a nearby friend
>> than a distant family.

Galatians 5:22

> But what happens when we live God's way? He brings gifts into our lives, much the same way that fruit appears in an orchard — things like affection for others, exuberance about life, serenity. We develop a willingness to stick with things, a sense of compassion in the heart, and a conviction that a basic holiness permeates things and people. We find ourselves involved in loyal commitments.

Mark 12:31b

> "'Love others as well as you love yourself.' There is no other commandment that ranks with these."

1 Corinthians 13:1-7

If I speak with human eloquence and angelic ecstasy but don't love, I'm nothing but the creaking of a rusty gate.

If I speak God's Word with power, revealing all his mysteries and making everything plain as day, and if I have faith that says to a mountain, "Jump," and it jumps, but I don't love, I'm nothing.

If I give everything I own to the poor and even go to the stake to be burned as a martyr, but I don't love, I've gotten nowhere. So, no matter what I say, what I believe, and what I do, I'm bankrupt without love.

Love never gives up.
Love cares more for others than for self.
Love doesn't want what it doesn't have.
Love doesn't strut,
Doesn't have a swelled head,
Doesn't force itself on others,
Isn't always "me first,"
Doesn't fly off the handle,
Doesn't keep score of the sins of others,

Doesn't revel when others grovel,

Takes pleasure in the flowering of truth,

Puts up with anything,

Trusts God always,

Always looks for the best,

Never looks back,

But keeps going to the end.

Luke 10:27

He said, "That you love the Lord your God with all your passion and prayer and muscle and intelligence — and that you love your neighbor as well as you do yourself."

Proverbs 25:25

Like a cool drink of water when you're worn out and weary is a letter from a long-lost friend.

Matthew 5:43-44

"You're familiar with the old written law, 'Love your friend,' and its unwritten companion, 'Hate your enemy.' I'm challenging that. I'm telling you to love your enemies. Let them bring out the best in you, not the worst. When someone gives you a hard time, respond with the energies of prayer."

1 John 4:7-11

My beloved friends, let us continue to love each other since love comes from God. Everyone who loves is born of God and experiences a relationship with God. The person who refuses to love doesn't know the first thing about God, because God *is* love — so you can't know him if you don't love. This is how God showed his love for us: God sent his only Son into the world so we might live through him. This is the kind of love we are talking about — not that we once upon a time loved God, but that he loved us and sent his Son as a sacrifice to clear away our sins and the damage they've done to our relationship with God.

My dear, dear friends, if God loved us like this, we certainly ought to love each other.

Proverbs 17:17

Friends love through all kinds of weather,
    and families stick together in all kinds of trouble.

Luke 10:25-37

Just then a religion scholar stood up with a question to test Jesus. "Teacher, what do I need to do to get eternal life?"

He answered, "What's written in God's Law? How do you interpret it?"

He said, "That you love the Lord your God with all your passion and prayer and muscle and intelligence — and that you love your neighbor as well as you do yourself."

"Good answer!" said Jesus. "Do it and you'll live."

Looking for a loophole, he asked, "And just how would you define 'neighbor'?"

Jesus answered by telling a story. "There was once a man traveling from Jerusalem to Jericho. On the way he was attacked by robbers. They took his clothes, beat him up, and went off leaving him half-dead. Luckily, a priest was on his way down the same road, but when he saw him he angled across to the other side. Then a Levite religious man showed up; he also avoided the injured man.

"A Samaritan traveling the road came on him. When he saw the man's condition, his heart went out to him. He gave him first aid, disinfecting and bandaging his wounds. Then he lifted him onto his donkey, led him to an inn, and made him comfortable. In the morning he took out two silver coins and gave them to the innkeeper, saying, 'Take good care of him. If it costs any more, put it on my bill—I'll pay you on my way back.'

"What do you think? Which of the three became a neighbor to the man attacked by robbers?"

"The one who treated him kindly," the religion scholar responded.

Jesus said, "Go and do the same."

Psalm 35:14

My prayers were like lead in my gut,
    like I'd lost my best friend, my brother.
I paced, distraught as a motherless child,
    hunched and heavyhearted.

John 13:34-35

"Let me give you a new command: Love one another. In the same way I loved you, you love one another. This is how everyone will recognize that you are my disciples — when they see the love you have for each other."

Hebrews 13:1-2

> Stay on good terms with each other, held together by love. Be
> ready with a meal or a bed when it's needed. Why, some have
> extended hospitality to angels without ever knowing it!

Colossians 3:13-14

> Be even-tempered, content with second place, quick to
> forgive an offense. Forgive as quickly and completely as the
> Master forgave you. And regardless of what else you put on,
> wear love. It's your basic, all-purpose garment. Never be
> without it.

Romans 12:9-21

> Love from the center of who you are; don't fake it. Run for
> dear life from evil; hold on for dear life to good. Be good
> friends who love deeply; practice playing second fiddle.
>
> Don't burn out; keep yourselves fueled and aflame. Be
> alert servants of the Master, cheerfully expectant. Don't quit
> in hard times; pray all the harder. Help needy Christians; be
> inventive in hospitality.
>
> Bless your enemies; no cursing under your breath.

Laugh with your happy friends when they're happy; share tears when they're down. Get along with each other; don't be stuck-up. Make friends with nobodies; don't be the great somebody.

Don't hit back; discover beauty in everyone. If you've got it in you, get along with everybody. Don't insist on getting even; that's not for you to do. "I'll do the judging," says God. "I'll take care of it."

Our Scriptures tell us that if you see your enemy hungry, go buy that person lunch, or if he's thirsty, get him a drink. Your generosity will surprise him with goodness. Don't let evil get the best of you; get the best of evil by doing good.

Psalm 36:10

Keep on loving your friends;
    do your work in welcoming hearts.

John 15:17

"But remember the root command: Love one another."

When they couldn't find a way in because of the
crowd, they went up on the roof, removed some tiles,
and let him down in the middle of everyone, right in
front of Jesus. Impressed by their bold belief, he said,
"Friend, I forgive your sins."

—LUKE 5:19-20

Stories *of* Friends

Psalm 16:3

> And these God-chosen lives all around —
> what splendid friends they make!

1 Samuel 18:1, *David and Jonathan*

By the time David had finished reporting to Saul, Jonathan was deeply impressed with David — an immediate bond was forged between them. He became totally committed to David. From that point on he would be David's number-one advocate and friend.

Ecclesiastes 4:12

> By yourself you're unprotected.
> With a friend you can face the worst.
> Can you round up a third?
> A three-stranded rope isn't easily snapped.

Ruth 1:16-18, *Ruth and Naomi*

> Ruth said, "Don't force me to leave you; don't make me go
> home. Where you go, I go; and where you live, I'll live. Your
> people are my people, your God is my god; where you die,
> I'll die, and that's where I'll be buried, so help me GOD —
> not even death itself is going to come between us!"
>
> When Naomi saw that Ruth had her heart set on going
> with her, she gave in. And so the two of them traveled on
> together to Bethlehem.

Job 42:10-11, *Job and his friends*

> After Job had interceded for his friends, GOD restored his
> fortune — and then doubled it! All his brothers and sisters
> and friends came to his house and celebrated. They told him
> how sorry they were, and consoled him for all the trouble

GOD had brought him. Each of them brought generous housewarming gifts.

1 Samuel 20:1-42, *David and Jonathan*

David got out of Naioth in Ramah alive and went to Jonathan. "What do I do now? What wrong have I inflicted on your father that makes him so determined to kill me?"

"Nothing," said Jonathan. "You've done nothing wrong. And you're not going to die. Really, you're not! My father tells me everything. He does nothing, whether big or little, without confiding in me. So why would he do this behind my back? It can't be."

But David said, "Your father knows that we are the best of friends. So he says to himself, 'Jonathan must know nothing of this. If he does, he'll side with David.' But it's true — as sure as GOD lives, and as sure as you're alive before me right now — he's determined to kill me."

Jonathan said, "Tell me what you have in mind. I'll do anything for you."

David said, "Tomorrow marks the New Moon. I'm scheduled to eat dinner with the king. Instead, I'll go hide in the field until the evening of the third. If your father misses me, say, 'David asked if he could run down to Bethlehem, his hometown, for an anniversary reunion, and worship with his family.' If he says, 'Good!' then I'm safe. But if he gets angry, you'll know for sure that he's made up his mind to kill me. Oh, stick with me in this. You've entered into a covenant of GOD with me, remember! If I'm in the wrong, go ahead and kill me yourself. Why bother giving me up to your father?"

"Never!" exclaimed Jonathan. "I'd never do that! If I get the slightest hint that my father is fixated on killing you, I'll tell you."

David asked, "And whom will you get to tell me if your father comes back with a harsh answer?"

"Come outside," said Jonathan. "Let's go to the field." When the two of them were out in the field, Jonathan said, "As GOD, the God of Israel, is my witness, by this time tomorrow I'll get it out of my father how he feels about you. Then I'll let you know what I learn. May GOD do his worst to me if I let you down! If my father still intends to kill you, I'll tell you and get you out of here in one piece. And GOD be with you as he's been with my father! If I make it through this alive, continue to be my covenant friend. And if I die, keep the covenant friendship with my family — forever. And when GOD finally rids the earth of David's enemies, stay loyal to Jonathan!" Jonathan repeated his pledge of love and friendship for David. He loved David more than his own soul!

Jonathan then laid out his plan: "Tomorrow is the New Moon, and you'll be missed when you don't show up for dinner. On the third day, when they've quit expecting you, come to the place where you hid before, and wait beside that big boulder. I'll shoot three arrows in the direction of the boulder. Then I'll send off my servant, 'Go find the arrows.' If I yell after the servant, 'The arrows are on this side! Retrieve them!' that's the signal that you can return safely — as GOD lives, not a thing to fear! But if I yell, 'The arrows are farther out!' then run for it — GOD wants you out of here! Regarding all the things we've discussed, remember that GOD's in on this with us to the very end!"

David hid in the field. On the holiday of the New Moon, the king came to the table to eat. He sat where he always sat, the place against the wall, with Jonathan across the table and Abner at Saul's side. But David's seat was empty. Saul didn't mention it at the time, thinking,

"Something's happened that's made him unclean. That's it—he's probably unclean for the holy meal."

But the day after the New Moon, day two of the holiday, David's seat was still empty. Saul asked Jonathan his son, "So where's that son of Jesse? He hasn't eaten with us either yesterday or today."

Jonathan said, "David asked my special permission to go to Bethlehem. He said, 'Give me leave to attend a family reunion back home. My brothers have ordered me to be there. If it seems all right to you, let me go and see my brothers.' That's why he's not here at the king's table."

Saul exploded in anger at Jonathan: "You son of a slut! Don't you think I know that you're in cahoots with the son of Jesse, disgracing both you and your mother? For as long as the son of Jesse is walking around free on this earth, your future in this kingdom is at risk. Now go get him. Bring him here. From this moment, he's as good as dead!"

Jonathan stood up to his father. "Why dead? What's he done?"

Saul threw his spear at him to kill him. That convinced Jonathan that his father was fixated on killing David.

Jonathan stormed from the table, furiously angry, and

ate nothing the rest of the day, upset for David and smart-
ing under the humiliation from his father.

In the morning, Jonathan went to the field for the
appointment with David. He had his young servant with him.
He told the servant, "Run and get the arrows I'm about to
shoot." The boy started running and Jonathan shot an arrow
way beyond him. As the boy came to the area where the
arrow had been shot, Jonathan yelled out, "Isn't the arrow
farther out?" He yelled again, "Hurry! Quickly! Don't just
stand there!" Jonathan's servant then picked up the arrow
and brought it to his master. The boy, of course, knew nothing of what was going on. Only Jonathan and David knew.

Jonathan gave his quiver and bow to the boy and sent
him back to town. After the servant was gone, David got
up from his hiding place beside the boulder, then fell on his
face to the ground — three times prostrating himself! And
then they kissed one another and wept, friend over friend,
David weeping especially hard.

Jonathan said, "Go in peace! The two of us have vowed
friendship in GOD's name, saying, 'GOD will be the bond
between me and you, and between my children and your
children forever!'"

Acts 15:35-36

> Paul and Barnabas stayed on in Antioch, teaching and preaching the Word of God. But they weren't alone. There were a number of teachers and preachers at that time in Antioch.
>
> After a few days of this, Paul said to Barnabas, "Let's go back and visit all our friends in each of the towns where we preached the Word of God. Let's see how they're doing."

Acts 28:14-15, *Luke and his friends*

> We found Christian friends there and stayed with them for a week.
>
> And then we came to Rome. Friends in Rome heard we were on the way and came out to meet us. One group got as far as Appian Court; another group met us at Three Taverns — emotion-packed meetings, as you can well imagine. Paul, brimming over with praise, led us in prayers of thanksgiving.

Acts 9:19-30, *Saul and his friends*

> Saul spent a few days getting acquainted with the Damascus disciples, but then went right to work, wasting no time,

preaching in the meeting places that this Jesus was the Son of God. They were caught off guard by this and, not at all sure they could trust him, they kept saying, "Isn't this the man who wreaked havoc in Jerusalem among the believers? And didn't he come here to do the same thing — arrest us and drag us off to jail in Jerusalem for sentencing by the high priests?"

But their suspicions didn't slow Saul down for even a minute. His momentum was up now and he plowed straight into the opposition, disarming the Damascus Jews and trying to show them that this Jesus was the Messiah.

After this had gone on quite a long time, some Jews conspired to kill him, but Saul got wind of it. They were watching the city gates around the clock so they could kill him. Then one night the disciples engineered his escape by lowering him over the wall in a basket.

Back in Jerusalem he tried to join the disciples, but they were all afraid of him. They didn't trust him one bit. Then Barnabas took him under his wing. He introduced him to the apostles and stood up for him, told them how Saul had seen and spoken to the Master on the Damascus Road and how in Damascus itself he had laid his life on the line with his bold preaching in Jesus' name.

After that he was accepted as one of them, going in and out of Jerusalem with no questions asked, uninhibited as he preached in the Master's name. But then he ran afoul of a group called Hellenists — he had been engaged in a running argument with them — who plotted his murder. When his friends learned of the plot, they got him out of town, took him to Caesarea, and then shipped him off to Tarsus.

Proverbs 25:11-13

The right word at the right time
is like a custom-made piece of jewelry,
And a wise friend's timely reprimand
is like a gold ring slipped on your finger.

Reliable friends who do what they say
are like cool drinks in sweltering heat — refreshing!

Philippians 2:19-30, *Paul and Timothy*

I plan (according to Jesus' plan) to send Timothy to you very soon so he can bring back all the news of you he can gather. Oh, how that will do my heart good! I have no one quite like Timothy. He is loyal, and genuinely concerned for you. Most people around here are looking out for themselves, with little concern for the things of Jesus. But you know yourselves that Timothy's the real thing. He's been a devoted son to me as together we've delivered the Message. As soon as I see how things are going to fall out for me here, I plan to send him off. And then I'm hoping and praying to be right on his heels.

But for right now, I'm dispatching Epaphroditus, my good friend and companion in my work. You sent him to help me out; now I'm sending him to help you out. He has been wanting in the worst way to get back with you. Especially since recovering from the illness you heard about, he's been wanting to get back and reassure you that he is just fine. He nearly died, as you know, but God had mercy on him. And not only on him—he had mercy on me, too. His death would have been one huge grief piled on top of all the others.

So you can see why I'm so delighted to send him on to you. When you see him again, hale and hearty, how you'll rejoice and how relieved I'll be. Give him a grand welcome, a joyful embrace! People like him deserve the best you can give. Remember the ministry to me that you started but weren't able to complete? Well, in the process of finishing up that work, he put his life on the line and nearly died doing it.

Acts 15:32-33, *Judas, Silas, and their friends*

Judas and Silas, good preachers both of them, strengthened their new friends with many words of courage and hope. Then it was time to go home. They were sent off by their new friends with laughter and embraces all around to report back to those who had sent them.

Matthew 5:23-24

"This is how I want you to conduct yourself in these matters. If you enter your place of worship and, about to make an offering, you suddenly remember a grudge a friend has against you, abandon your offering, leave immediately, go to this friend and make things right. Then and only then, come back and work things out with God."

2 Timothy 1:16-18, *Paul and Onesiphorus*

But God bless Onesiphorus and his family! Many's the time I've been refreshed in that house. And he wasn't embarrassed a bit that I was in jail. The first thing he did when he got to Rome was look me up. May God on the Last Day treat him as well as he treated me. And then there was all the help he provided in Ephesus—but you know that better than I.

Job 2:11-13, *Job and his friends*

Three of Job's friends heard of all the trouble that had fallen on him. Each traveled from his own country—Eliphaz from Teman, Bildad from Shuhah, Zophar from Naamath—and went together to Job to keep him company and comfort him. When they first caught sight of him, they couldn't believe what they saw—they hardly recognized him! They cried out in lament, ripped their robes, and dumped dirt on their heads as a sign of their grief. Then they sat with him on the ground. Seven days and nights they sat there without saying a word. They could see how rotten he felt, how deeply he was suffering.

Acts 12:1-17, *Peter and his friends*

That's when King Herod got it into his head to go after some of the church members. He murdered James, John's brother. When he saw how much it raised his popularity ratings with the Jews, he arrested Peter—all this during Passover Week, mind you—and had him thrown in jail, putting four squads of four soldiers each to guard him. He was planning a public lynching after Passover.

All the time that Peter was under heavy guard in the jailhouse, the church prayed for him most strenuously.

Then the time came for Herod to bring him out for the kill. That night, even though shackled to two soldiers, one on either side, Peter slept like a baby. And there were guards at the door keeping their eyes on the place. Herod was taking no chances!

Suddenly there was an angel at his side and light flooding the room. The angel shook Peter and got him up: "Hurry!" The handcuffs fell off his wrists. The angel said, "Get dressed. Put on your shoes." Peter did it. Then, "Grab your coat and let's get out of here." Peter followed him, but didn't believe it was really an angel—he thought he was dreaming.

Past the first guard and then the second, they came to the iron gate that led into the city. It swung open before them on its own, and they were out on the street, free as the breeze. At the first intersection the angel left him, going his own way. That's when Peter realized it was no dream. "I can't believe it — this really happened! The Master sent his angel and rescued me from Herod's vicious little production and the spectacle the Jewish mob was looking forward to."

Still shaking his head, amazed, he went to Mary's house, the Mary who was John Mark's mother. The house was packed with praying friends. When he knocked on the door to the courtyard, a young woman named Rhoda came to see who it was. But when she recognized his voice — Peter's voice! — she was so excited and eager to tell everyone Peter was there that she forgot to open the door and left him standing in the street.

But they wouldn't believe her, dismissing her, dismissing her report. "You're crazy," they said. She stuck by her story, insisting. They still wouldn't believe her and said, "It must be his angel." All this time poor Peter was standing out in the street, knocking away.

Finally they opened up and saw him — and went

wild! Peter put his hands up and calmed them down. He described how the Master had gotten him out of jail, then said, "Tell James and the brothers what's happened." He left them and went off to another place.

Proverbs 18:24

Friends come and friends go,
   but a true friend sticks by you like family.

Now, friends, read these next words carefully.
Slow down and don't go jumping to conclusions
regarding the day when our Master, Jesus Christ,
will come back and we assemble to welcome him.

—2 THESSALONIANS 2:1

So, friends, take a firm stand,

feet on the ground and head high.

Keep a tight grip on what you were taught,

whether in personal conversation or by our letter.

—2 Thessalonians 2:15

ADVICE *for* MY FRIENDS

Proverbs 27:17

> You use steel to sharpen steel,
>> and one friend sharpens another.

Proverbs 4:20-27

> Dear friend, listen well to my words;
>> tune your ears to my voice.
> Keep my message in plain view at all times.
>> Concentrate! Learn it by heart!
> Those who discover these words live, really live;
>> body and soul, they're bursting with health.
> Keep vigilant watch over your heart;
>> *that's* where life starts.
> Don't talk out of both sides of your mouth;

avoid careless banter, white lies, and gossip.
Keep your eyes straight ahead;
  ignore all sideshow distractions.
Watch your step,
  and the road will stretch out smooth before you.
Look neither right nor left;
  leave evil in the dust.

Galatians 5:22-23a

But what happens when we live God's way? He brings gifts
into our lives, much the same way that fruit appears in an
orchard — things like affection for others, exuberance about
life, serenity. We develop a willingness to stick with things,
a sense of compassion in the heart, and a conviction that a
basic holiness permeates things and people. We find ourselves involved in loyal commitments, not needing to force
our way in life, able to marshal and direct our energies wisely.

Proverbs 27:14

If you wake your friend in the early morning
  by shouting "Rise and shine!"

It will sound to him
more like a curse than a blessing.

Proverbs 25:17

And when you find a friend, don't outwear your welcome;
show up at all hours and he'll soon get fed up.

Luke 17:3-4

"Be alert. If you see your friend going wrong, correct him.
If he responds, forgive him. Even if it's personal against you
and repeated seven times through the day, and seven times
he says, 'I'm sorry, I won't do it again,' forgive him."

Acts 13:26

"Dear brothers and sisters, children of Abraham, and
friends of God, this message of salvation has been precisely
targeted to you."

James 1:19

> Post this at all the intersections, dear friends: Lead with
> your ears, follow up with your tongue, and let anger straggle
> along in the rear.

Proverbs 3:13-14

> You're blessed when you meet Lady Wisdom,
>> when you make friends with Madame Insight.
> She's worth far more than money in the bank;
>> her friendship is better than a big salary.

Proverbs 1:10-19

> Dear friend, if bad companions tempt you,
>> don't go along with them.
> If they say — "Let's go out and raise some hell.
>> Let's beat up some old man, mug some old woman.
> Let's pick them clean
>> and get them ready for their funerals.
> We'll load up on top-quality loot.
>> We'll haul it home by the truckload.
> Join us for the time of your life!

With us, it's share and share alike!" —
Oh, friend, don't give them a second look;
   don't listen to them for a minute.
They're racing to a very bad end,
   hurrying to ruin everything they lay hands on.
Nobody robs a bank
   with everyone watching,
Yet that's what these people are doing —
   they're doing themselves in.
When you grab all you can get, that's what happens:
   the more you get, the less you are.

3 John 1:2

We're the best of friends, and I pray for good fortune in everything you do, and for your good health — that your everyday affairs prosper, as well as your soul!

2 Peter 1:5-11

So don't lose a minute in building on what you've been given, complementing your basic faith with good character, spiritual understanding, alert discipline, passionate

patience, reverent wonder, warm friendliness, and generous love, each dimension fitting into and developing the
others. With these qualities active and growing in your
lives, no grass will grow under your feet, no day will pass
without its reward as you mature in your experience of our
Master Jesus. Without these qualities you can't see what's
right before you, oblivious that your old sinful life has been
wiped off the books.

So, friends, confirm God's invitation to you, his choice
of you. Don't put it off; do it now. Do this, and you'll have
your life on a firm footing, the streets paved and the way
wide open into the eternal kingdom of our Master and
Savior, Jesus Christ.

Proverbs 16:27-28

Mean people spread mean gossip;
their words smart and burn.

Troublemakers start fights;
gossips break up friendships.

Proverbs 6:20-23

> Good friend, follow your father's good advice;
>> don't wander off from your mother's teachings.
> Wrap yourself in them from head to foot;
>> wear them like a scarf around your neck.
> Wherever you walk, they'll guide you;
>> whenever you rest, they'll guard you;
>> when you wake up, they'll tell you what's next.
> For sound advice is a beacon,
>> good teaching is a light,
>> moral discipline is a life path.

2 Thessalonians 2:13

> Meanwhile, we've got our hands full continually thanking God for you, our good friends — so loved by God! God picked you out as his from the very start. Think of it: included in God's original plan of salvation by the bond of faith in the living truth.

Hebrews 10:19-25

So, friends, we can now — without hesitation — walk right up to God, into "the Holy Place." Jesus has cleared the way by the blood of his sacrifice, acting as our priest before God. The "curtain" into God's presence is his body.

So let's *do* it — full of belief, confident that we're presentable inside and out. Let's keep a firm grip on the promises that keep us going. He always keeps his word. Let's see how inventive we can be in encouraging love and helping out, not avoiding worshiping together as some do but spurring each other on, especially as we see the big Day approaching.

Proverbs 7:1-4

Dear friend, do what I tell you;
    treasure my careful instructions.
Do what I say and you'll live well.
    My teaching is as precious as your eyesight — guard it!
Write it out on the back of your hands;
    etch it on the chambers of your heart.
Talk to Wisdom as to a sister.
    Treat Insight as your companion.

Proverbs 2:1-5

> Good friend, take to heart what I'm telling you;
>> collect my counsels and guard them with your life.
> Tune your ears to the world of Wisdom;
>> set your heart on a life of Understanding.
> That's right — if you make Insight your priority,
>> and won't take no for an answer,
> Searching for it like a prospector panning for gold,
>> like an adventurer on a treasure hunt,
> Believe me, before you know it Fear-of-GOD will be yours;
>> you'll have come upon the Knowledge of God.

Hebrews 3:12-13

> So watch your step, friends. Make sure there's no evil unbelief lying around that will trip you up and throw you off course, diverting you from the living God. For as long as it's still God's Today, keep each other on your toes so sin doesn't slow down your reflexes.

Proverbs 6:1-5

> Dear friend, if you've gone into hock with your neighbor
>> or locked yourself into a deal with a stranger,

If you've impulsively promised the shirt off your back
  and now find yourself shivering out in the cold,
Friend, don't waste a minute, get yourself out of that mess.
    You're in that man's clutches!
    Go, put on a long face; act desperate.
Don't procrastinate —
    there's no time to lose.
Run like a deer from the hunter,
    fly like a bird from the trapper!

Proverbs 4:10-15

Dear friend, take my advice;
    it will add years to your life.
I'm writing out clear directions to Wisdom Way,
    I'm drawing a map to Righteous Road.
I don't want you ending up in blind alleys,
    or wasting time making wrong turns.
Hold tight to good advice; don't relax your grip.
    Guard it well — your life is at stake!
Don't take Wicked Bypass;
    don't so much as set foot on that road.

Stay clear of it; give it a wide berth.

Make a detour and be on your way.

Psalm 78:1-4

Listen, dear friends, to God's truth,

bend your ears to what I tell you.

I'm chewing on the morsel of a proverb;

I'll let you in on the sweet old truths,

Stories we heard from our fathers,

counsel we learned at our mother's knee.

We're not keeping this to ourselves,

we're passing it along to the next generation —

GOD's fame and fortune,

the marvelous things he has done.

Luke 12:22-32

He continued this subject with his disciples. "Don't fuss
about what's on the table at mealtimes or if the clothes in
your closet are in fashion. There is far more to your inner
life than the food you put in your stomach, more to your
outer appearance than the clothes you hang on your body.

Look at the ravens, free and unfettered, not tied down to a job description, carefree in the care of God. And you count far more.

"Has anyone by fussing before the mirror ever gotten taller by so much as an inch? If fussing can't even do that, why fuss at all? Walk into the fields and look at the wildflowers. They don't fuss with their appearance — but have you ever seen color and design quite like it? The ten best-dressed men and women in the country look shabby alongside them. If God gives such attention to the wildflowers, most of them never even seen, don't you think he'll attend to you, take pride in you, do his best for you?

"What I'm trying to do here is get you to relax, not be so preoccupied with *getting* so you can respond to God's *giving*. People who don't know God and the way he works fuss over these things, but you know both God and how he works. Steep yourself in God-reality, God-initiative, God-provisions. You'll find all your everyday human concerns will be met. Don't be afraid of missing out. You're my dearest friends! The Father wants to give you the very kingdom itself."

Proverbs 4:1-9

Listen, friends, to some fatherly advice;
>   sit up and take notice so you'll know how to live.
I'm giving you good counsel;
>   don't let it go in one ear and out the other.

When I was a boy at my father's knee,
>   the pride and joy of my mother,
He would sit me down and drill me:
>   "Take this to heart. Do what I tell you — live!
Sell everything and buy Wisdom! Forage for Understanding!
>   Don't forget one word! Don't deviate an inch!
Never walk away from Wisdom — she guards your life;
>   love her — she keeps her eye on you.
Above all and before all, do this: Get Wisdom!
>   Write this at the top of your list: Get Understanding!
Throw your arms around her — believe me, you won't regret it;
>   never let her go — she'll make your life glorious.
She'll garland your life with grace,
>   she'll festoon your days with beauty."

Proverbs 2:10-12

> Lady Wisdom will be your close friend,
>   and Brother Knowledge your pleasant companion.
> Good Sense will scout ahead for danger,
>   Insight will keep an eye out for you.
> They'll keep you from making wrong turns,
>   or following the bad directions.

James 2:14-18

> Dear friends, do you think you'll get anywhere in this if
> you learn all the right words but never do anything? Does
> merely talking about faith indicate that a person really
> has it? For instance, you come upon an old friend dressed
> in rags and half-starved and say, "Good morning, friend!
> Be clothed in Christ! Be filled with the Holy Spirit!" and
> walk off without providing so much as a coat or a cup of
> soup — where does that get you? Isn't it obvious that God-
> talk without God-acts is outrageous nonsense?
>
> I can already hear one of you agreeing by saying,
> "Sounds good. You take care of the faith department, I'll
> handle the works department."

Not so fast. You can no more show me your works apart from your faith than I can show you my faith apart from my works. Faith and works, works and faith, fit together hand in glove.

Proverbs 1:7-9

Start with GOD—the first step in learning is bowing down
    to GOD;
    only fools thumb their noses at such wisdom and learning.

Pay close attention, friend, to what your father tells you;
    never forget what you learned at your mother's knee.
Wear their counsel like flowers in your hair,
    like rings on your fingers.

Proverbs 3:21

Dear friend, guard Clear Thinking and Common Sense
    with your life;
    don't for a minute lose sight of them.
They'll keep your soul alive and well,
    they'll keep you fit and attractive.
You'll travel safely,

you'll neither tire nor trip.
You'll take afternoon naps without a worry,
    you'll enjoy a good night's sleep.
No need to panic over alarms or surprises,
    or predictions that doomsday's just around the corner,
Because GOD will be right there with you;
    he'll keep you safe and sound.

Acts 13:38

"I want you to know, my very dear friends, that it is on
account of this resurrected Jesus that the forgiveness of
your sins can be promised."

Philippians 4:1

My dear, dear friends! I love you so much. I do want the
very best for you. You make me feel such joy, fill me with
such pride. Don't waver. Stay on track, steady in God.

Proverbs 3:1-12

Good friend, don't forget all I've taught you;
    take to heart my commands.

They'll help you live a long, long time,
    a long life lived full and well.

Don't lose your grip on Love and Loyalty.
    Tie them around your neck; carve their initials on your
        heart.
Earn a reputation for living well
    in God's eyes and the eyes of the people.

Trust GOD from the bottom of your heart;
    don't try to figure out everything on your own.
Listen for GOD's voice in everything you do, everywhere
    you go;
    he's the one who will keep you on track.
Don't assume that you know it all.
    Run to GOD! Run from evil!
Your body will glow with health,
    your very bones will vibrate with life!
Honor GOD with everything you own;
    give him the first and the best.
Your barns will burst,
    your wine vats will brim over.

But don't, dear friend, resent GOD's discipline;
>   don't sulk under his loving correction.
It's the child he loves that GOD corrects;
>   a father's delight is behind all this.

Romans 16:17-20

One final word of counsel, friends. Keep a sharp eye out
for those who take bits and pieces of the teaching that you
learned and then use them to make trouble. Give these
people a wide berth. They have no intention of living for
our Master Christ. They're only in this for what they can
get out of it, and aren't above using pious sweet talk to dupe
unsuspecting innocents.

And so while there has never been any question about
your honesty in these matters — I couldn't be more proud
of you! — I want you also to be smart, making sure every
"good" thing is the *real* thing. Don't be gullible in regard
to smooth-talking evil. Stay alert like this, and before you
know it the God of peace will come down on Satan with
both feet, stomping him into the dirt. Enjoy the best of
Jesus!

*Friends, when life gets really difficult,
don't jump to the conclusion that God
isn't on the job. Instead, be glad that you are
in the very thick of what Christ experienced.
This is a spiritual refining process,
with glory just around the corner.*

—1 PETER 4:12-13

Friends, this world is not your home,

so don't make yourselves cozy in it.

Don't indulge your ego at

the expense of your soul.

—1 PETER 2:11

Husbands and Wives
As Friends

Song of Songs 1:15

The Man
Oh, my dear friend! You're so beautiful!
And your eyes so beautiful — like doves!

Song of Songs 4:9-10

The Man
You've captured my heart, dear friend.
    You looked at me, and I fell in love.
    One look my way and I was hopelessly in love!
How beautiful your love, dear, dear friend —
    far more pleasing than a fine, rare wine,
    your fragrance more exotic than select spices.

Song of Songs 2:2

> THE MAN
> A lotus blossoming in a swamp of weeds —
>> that's my dear friend among the girls in the village.

Songs of Songs 2:8-10

> THE WOMAN
> Look! Listen! There's my lover!
>> Do you see him coming?
> Vaulting the mountains,
>> leaping the hills.
> My lover is like a gazelle, graceful;
>> like a young stag, virile.
> Look at him there, on tiptoe at the gate,
>> all ears, all eyes — ready!
> My lover has arrived
>> and he's speaking to me!

> THE MAN
> Get up, my dear friend,
>> fair and beautiful lover — come to me!

Ruth 2:8-16; 3:1-13; 4:13

Then Boaz spoke to Ruth: "Listen, my daughter. From now on don't go to any other field to glean — stay right here in this one. And stay close to my young women. Watch where they are harvesting and follow them. And don't worry about a thing; I've given orders to my servants not to harass you. When you get thirsty, feel free to go and drink from the water buckets that the servants have filled."

She dropped to her knees, then bowed her face to the ground. "How does this happen that you should pick me out and treat me so kindly — *me*, a foreigner?"

Boaz answered her, "I've heard all about you — heard about the way you treated your mother-in-law after the death of her husband, and how you left your father and mother and the land of your birth and have come to live among a bunch of total strangers. GOD reward you well for what you've done — and with a generous bonus besides from GOD, to whom you've come seeking protection under his wings."

She said, "Oh sir, such grace, such kindness — I don't deserve it. You've touched my heart, treated me like one of your own. And I don't even belong here!"

At the lunch break, Boaz said to her, "Come over here; eat some bread. Dip it in the wine."

So she joined the harvesters. Boaz passed the roasted grain to her. She ate her fill and even had some left over.

When she got up to go back to work, Boaz ordered his servants: "Let her glean where there's still plenty of grain on the ground — make it easy for her. Better yet, pull some of the good stuff out and leave it for her to glean. Give her special treatment." . . .

One day her mother-in-law Naomi said to Ruth, "My dear daughter, isn't it about time I arranged a good home for you so you can have a happy life? And isn't Boaz our close relative, the one with whose young women you've been working? Maybe it's time to make our move. Tonight is the night of Boaz's barley harvest at the threshing floor.

"Take a bath. Put on some perfume. Get all dressed up and go to the threshing floor. But don't let him know you're there until the party is well under way and he's had plenty of food and drink. When you see him slipping off to sleep, watch where he lies down and then go there. Lie at his feet to let him know that you are available to him for marriage. Then wait and see what he says. He'll tell you what to do."

Ruth said, "If you say so, I'll do it, just as you've told me."

She went down to the threshing floor and put her mother-in-law's plan into action.

Boaz had a good time, eating and drinking his fill—he felt great. Then he went off to get some sleep, lying down at the end of a stack of barley. Ruth quietly followed; she lay down to signal her availability for marriage.

In the middle of the night the man was suddenly startled and sat up. Surprise! This woman asleep at his feet!

He said, "And who are you?"

She said, "I am Ruth, your maiden; take me under your protecting wing. You're my close relative, you know, in the circle of covenant redeemers — you do have the right to marry me."

He said, "GOD bless you, my dear daughter! What a splendid expression of love! And when you could have had your pick of any of the young men around. And now, my dear daughter, don't you worry about a thing; I'll do all you could want or ask. Everybody in town knows what a courageous woman you are — a real prize! You're right, I am a close relative to you, but there is one even closer than I am.

So stay the rest of the night. In the morning, if he wants
to exercise his customary rights and responsibilities as the
closest covenant redeemer, he'll have his chance; but if he
isn't interested, as GOD lives, I'll do it. Now go back to
sleep until morning." . . .

Boaz married Ruth. She became his wife. Boaz slept with
her. By GOD's gracious gift she conceived and had a son.

Ephesians 5:22-28

Wives, understand and support your husbands in ways that
show your support for Christ. The husband provides leadership to his wife the way Christ does to his church, not by
domineering but by cherishing. So just as the church sub-
mits to Christ as he exercises such leadership, wives should
likewise submit to their husbands.

Husbands, go all out in your love for your wives, exactly
as Christ did for the church — a love marked by giving, not
getting. Christ's love makes the church whole. His words
evoke her beauty. Everything he does and says is designed to
bring the best out of her, dressing her in dazzling white silk,
radiant with holiness. And that is how husbands ought to

love their wives. They're really doing themselves a favor —
since they're already "one" in marriage.

Ecclesiastes 4:7-9

I turned my head and saw yet another wisp of smoke on its
way to nothingness: a solitary person, completely alone —
no children, no family, no friends — yet working obsessively
late into the night, compulsively greedy for more and more,
never bothering to ask, "Why am I working like a dog,
never having any fun? And who cares?" More smoke. A bad
business.

It's better to have a partner than go it alone.
Share the work, share the wealth.

Proverbs 5:18-19

Bless your fresh-flowing fountain!
Enjoy the wife you married as a young man!
Lovely as an angel, beautiful as a rose —
don't ever quit taking delight in her body.
Never take her love for granted!

Songs of Songs 6:3-9

> THE WOMAN
>
> I am my lover's and my lover is mine.
>
>> He caresses the sweet-smelling flowers.
>
> THE MAN
>
> Dear, dear friend and lover,
>
>> you're as beautiful as Tirzah, city of delights,
>
> Lovely as Jerusalem, city of dreams,
>
>> the ravishing visions of my ecstasy.
>
> Your beauty is too much for me — I'm in over my head.
>
>> I'm not used to this! I can't take it in.
>
> Your hair flows and shimmers
>
>> like a flock of goats in the distance
>>
>> streaming down a hillside in the sunshine.
>
> Your smile is generous and full —
>
>> expressive and strong and clean.
>
> Your veiled cheeks
>
>> are soft and radiant.
>
> There's no one like her on earth,
>
>> never has been, never will be.

She's a woman beyond compare.

 My dove is perfection,

Pure and innocent as the day she was born,

 and cradled in joy by her mother.

Everyone who came by to see her

 exclaimed and admired her —

All the fathers and mothers, the neighbors and friends,

 blessed and praised her.

Songs of Songs 2:13-14

THE MAN

Lilacs are exuberantly purple and perfumed,

 and cherry trees fragrant with blossoms.

Oh, get up, dear friend,

 my fair and beautiful lover — come to me!

Come, my shy and modest dove —

 leave your seclusion, come out in the open.

Let me see your face,

 let me hear your voice.

For your voice is soothing

 and your face is ravishing.

Songs of Songs 5:1-2

THE MAN
I went to my garden, dear friend, best lover!
 breathed the sweet fragrance.
I ate the fruit and honey,
 I drank the nectar and wine.

Celebrate with me, friends!
 Raise your glasses — "To life! To love!"

THE WOMAN
I was sound asleep, but in my dreams I was wide awake.
 Oh, listen! It's the sound of my lover knocking, calling!

THE MAN
"Let me in, dear companion, dearest friend,
 my dove, consummate lover!
I'm soaked with the dampness of the night,
 drenched with dew, shivering and cold."

Song of Songs 4:12

> THE MAN
> Dear lover and friend, you're a secret garden,
>> a private and pure fountain.

Ecclesiastes 4:11

> Two in a bed warm each other.
> Alone, you shiver all night.

I thank you always

that you went into action.

And I'll stay right here,

your good name my hope,

in company with your faithful friends.

—PSALM 52:9

FRIENDSHIP WITH GOD

Psalm 34:15

> GOD keeps an eye on his friends,
> his ears pick up every moan and groan.

Psalm 25:12-14

> My question: What are God-worshipers like?
> Your answer: Arrows aimed at God's bull's-eye.
>
> They settle down in a promising place;
> Their kids inherit a prosperous farm.
>
> God-friendship is for God-worshipers;
> They are the ones he confides in.

Job 1:8

> GOD said to Satan, "Have you noticed my friend Job?
> There's no one quite like him — honest and true to his
> word, totally devoted to God and hating evil."

Job 2:3

> Then GOD said to Satan, "Have you noticed my friend Job?
> There's no one quite like him, is there — honest and true to
> his word, totally devoted to God and hating evil? He still
> has a firm grip on his integrity! You tried to trick me into
> destroying him, but it didn't work."

1 Chronicles 29:17

> "I know, dear God, that you care nothing for the surface —
> you want *us*, our true selves — and so I have given from the
> heart, honestly and happily. And now see all these people
> doing the same, giving freely, willingly — what a joy!"

Romans 5:9-11

> Now that we are set right with God by means of this sac-
> rificial death, the consummate blood sacrifice, there is no

longer a question of being at odds with God in any way.
If, when we were at our worst, we were put on friendly
terms with God by the sacrificial death of his Son, now that
we're at our best, just think of how our lives will expand
and deepen by means of his resurrection life! Now that we
have actually received this amazing friendship with God,
we are no longer content to simply say it in plodding prose.
We sing and shout our praises to God through Jesus, the
Messiah!

Matthew 18:19-20

"When two of you get together on anything at all on earth
and make a prayer of it, my Father in heaven goes into
action. And when two or three of you are together because
of me, you can be sure that I'll be there."

Psalm 37:27-28

Turn your back on evil,
    work for the good and don't quit.
GOD loves this kind of thing,
    never turns away from his friends.

Live this way and you've got it made,
    but bad eggs will be tossed out.

Proverbs 8:32-36

"So, my dear friends, listen carefully;
    those who embrace these my ways are most blessed.
Mark a life of discipline and live wisely;
    don't squander your precious life.
Blessed the man, blessed the woman, who listens to me,
    awake and ready for me each morning,
    alert and responsive as I start my day's work.
When you find me, you find life, real life,
    to say nothing of GOD's good pleasure.
But if you wrong me, you damage your very soul;
    when you reject me, you're flirting with death."

John 14:16-17

"I will talk to the Father, and he'll provide you another
Friend so that you will always have someone with you. This
Friend is the Spirit of Truth. The godless world can't take
him in because it doesn't have eyes to see him, doesn't know

what to look for. But you know him already because he has been staying with you, and will even be *in* you!"

Psalm 63:11

> But the king is glad in God;
>> his true friends spread the joy,
> While small-minded gossips
>> are gagged for good.

2 Corinthians 5:20

> We're Christ's representatives. God uses us to persuade men and women to drop their differences and enter into God's work of making things right between them. We're speaking for Christ himself now: Become friends with God; he's already a friend with you.

John 14:26

> "The Friend, the Holy Spirit whom the Father will send at my request, will make everything plain to you. He will remind you of all the things I have told you."

2 Corinthians 13:14

> The amazing grace of the Master, Jesus Christ, the extravagant love of God, the intimate friendship of the Holy Spirit, be with all of you.

You talk about GOD, the God-of-the-Angel-Armies,

being your best friend.

Well, live like it,

and maybe it will happen.

—AMOS 5:14

I have one request, dear friends:
Pray for me. Pray strenuously with
and for me—to God the Father,
through the power of our Master Jesus,
through the love of the Spirit.

—ROMANS 15:30

How to Treat Your Friends

Luke 6:36

"Our Father is kind; you be kind."

Ephesians 5:21

Out of respect for Christ, be courteously reverent to one another.

Matthew 7:1-5

"Don't pick on people, jump on their failures, criticize their faults — unless, of course, you want the same treatment. That critical spirit has a way of boomeranging. It's easy to see a smudge on your neighbor's face and be oblivious to the ugly sneer on your own. Do you have the nerve to say, 'Let me wash your face for you,' when your own face is distorted by contempt? It's this whole traveling road-show mentality all over again, playing a holier-than-thou part instead of just living your part. Wipe that ugly sneer off your own face, and you might be fit to offer a washcloth to your neighbor."

1 Samuel 2:9

He protectively cares for his faithful friends, step by step,
but leaves the wicked to stumble in the dark.
No one makes it in this life by sheer muscle!

Proverbs 14:21

It's criminal to ignore a neighbor in need,
    but compassion for the poor—what a blessing!

Romans 12:20

Our Scriptures tell us that if you see your enemy hungry,
go buy that person lunch, or if he's thirsty, get him a drink.
Your generosity will surprise him with goodness.

Philippians 2:1-4

> If you've gotten anything at all out of following Christ, if
> his love has made any difference in your life, if being in
> a community of the Spirit means anything to you, if you
> have a heart, if you *care* — then do me a favor: Agree with
> each other, love each other, be deep-spirited friends. Don't
> push your way to the front; don't sweet-talk your way to the
> top. Put yourself aside, and help others get ahead. Don't be
> obsessed with getting your own advantage. Forget yourselves
> long enough to lend a helping hand.

Zechariah 7:9

> "Well, the message hasn't changed. GOD-of-the-Angel-
> Armies said then and says now:
>
> > "'Treat one another justly.
> > Love your neighbors.
> > Be compassionate with each other.'"

Luke 12:33-34

> "Be generous. Give to the poor. Get yourselves a bank that
> can't go bankrupt, a bank in heaven far from bankrobbers,

safe from embezzlers, a bank you can bank on. It's obvious, isn't it? The place where your treasure is, is the place you will most want to be, and end up being."

Galatians 6:2-5

Stoop down and reach out to those who are oppressed. Share their burdens, and so complete Christ's law. If you think you are too good for that, you are badly deceived.

Make a careful exploration of who you are and the work you have been given, and then sink yourself into that. Don't be impressed with yourself. Don't compare yourself with others. Each of you must take responsibility for doing the creative best you can with your own life.

Romans 15:7

So reach out and welcome one another to God's glory. Jesus did it; now *you* do it!

Galatians 5:13

It is absolutely clear that God has called you to a free life. Just make sure that you don't use this freedom as an excuse to do whatever you want to do and destroy your freedom. Rather, use your freedom to serve one another in love; that's how freedom grows.

Luke 11:5-9

Then he said, "Imagine what would happen if you went to a friend in the middle of the night and said, 'Friend, lend me three loaves of bread. An old friend traveling through just showed up, and I don't have a thing on hand.'

"The friend answers from his bed, 'Don't bother me. The door's locked; my children are all down for the night; I can't get up to give you anything.'

"But let me tell you, even if he won't get up because he's a friend, if you stand your ground, knocking and waking all the neighbors, he'll finally get up and get you whatever you need.

"Here's what I'm saying:

Ask and you'll get;
Seek and you'll find;
Knock and the door will open."

1 Corinthians 8:11-12

> Christ gave up his life for that person. Wouldn't you at least
> be willing to give up going to dinner for him — because,
> as you say, it doesn't really make any difference? But it *does*
> make a difference if you hurt your friend terribly, risking his
> eternal ruin! When you hurt your friend, you hurt Christ.
> A free meal here and there isn't worth it at the cost of even
> one of these "weak ones."

Proverbs 22:11

> GOD loves the pure-hearted and well-spoken;
>   good leaders also delight in their friendship.

Proverbs 18:19

> Do a favor and win a friend forever;
>   nothing can untie that bond.

1 Corinthians 1:10

> I have a serious concern to bring up with you, my friends,
> using the authority of Jesus, our Master. I'll put it as

urgently as I can: You *must* get along with each other. You must learn to be considerate of one another, cultivating a life in common.

1 Peter 3:8-9

Summing up: Be agreeable, be sympathetic, be loving, be compassionate, be humble. That goes for all of you, no exceptions. No retaliation. No sharp-tongued sarcasm. Instead, bless — that's your job, to bless. You'll be a blessing and also get a blessing.

Colossians 3:9

Don't lie to one another. You're done with that old life. It's like a filthy set of ill-fitting clothes you've stripped off and put in the fire.

James 4:11-12

Don't bad-mouth each other, friends. It's God's Word, his Message, his Royal Rule, that takes a beating in that kind of talk. You're supposed to be honoring the Message, not writing graffiti all over it. God is in charge of deciding human destiny. Who do you think you are to meddle in the destiny of others?

James 5:9

Friends, don't complain about each other. A far greater complaint could be lodged against you, you know. The Judge is standing just around the corner.

Ephesians 4:29

Watch the way you talk. Let nothing foul or dirty come out of your mouth. Say only what helps, each word a gift.

1 Thessalonians 5:11

So speak encouraging words to one another. Build up hope so you'll all be together in this, no one left out, no one left behind. I know you're already doing this; just keep on doing it.

Proverbs 14:10

> The person who shuns the bitter moments of friends
> will be an outsider at their celebrations.

Leviticus 19:10

> "Don't exploit your friend or rob him.
> "Don't hold back the wages of a hired hand overnight."

Acts 16:40

> Paul and Silas went straight to Lydia's house, saw their
> friends again, encouraged them in the faith, and only then
> went on their way.

Luke 6:28-31

> "When someone gives you a hard time, respond with the
> energies of prayer for that person. If someone slaps you in
> the face, stand there and take it. If someone grabs your shirt,
> giftwrap your best coat and make a present of it. If someone
> takes unfair advantage of you, use the occasion to practice the
> servant life. No more tit-for-tat stuff. Live generously.

"Here is a simple rule of thumb for behavior: Ask yourself what you want people to do for you; then grab the initiative and do it for *them!*"

Matthew 18:15-16

"If a fellow believer hurts you, go and tell him — work it out between the two of you. If he listens, you've made a friend. If he won't listen, take one or two others along so that the presence of witnesses will keep things honest, and try again."

Ephesians 4:32

Be gentle with one another, sensitive. Forgive one another as quickly and thoroughly as God in Christ forgave you.

James 5:16

Make this your common practice: Confess your sins to each other and pray for each other so that you can live together whole and healed. The prayer of a person living right with God is something powerful to be reckoned with.

Psalm 15:2-5

> "Walk straight,
>   act right,
>   tell the truth.

> "Don't hurt your friend,
>   don't blame your neighbor;
>   despise the despicable.

> "Keep your word even when it costs you,
>   make an honest living,
>   never take a bribe."

Matthew 25:34-40

"Then the King will say to those on his right, 'Enter, you who are blessed by my Father! Take what's coming to you in this kingdom. It's been ready for you since the world's foundation. And here's why:

> I was hungry and you fed me,
> I was thirsty and you gave me a drink,
> I was homeless and you gave me a room,

I was shivering and you gave me clothes,

I was sick and you stopped to visit,

I was in prison and you came to me.'

"Then those 'sheep' are going to say, 'Master, what are you talking about? When did we ever see you hungry and feed you, thirsty and give you a drink? And when did we ever see you sick or in prison and come to you?' Then the King will say, 'I'm telling the solemn truth: Whenever you did one of these things to someone overlooked or ignored, that was me — you did it to me.'"

So how should I prepare to come to you?
As a severe disciplinarian
who makes you toe the mark?
Or as a good friend and counselor
who wants to share heart-to-heart
with you? You decide.

—1 CORINTHIANS 4:21

"Please, my friends, come to my house
and stay the night. Wash up.
You can rise early and be
on your way refreshed."

—GENESIS 19:2

Jesus' Friends

Luke 22:31-33, *Jesus and Simon Peter*

"Simon, stay on your toes. Satan has tried his best to separate all of you from me, like chaff from wheat. Simon, I've prayed for you in particular that you not give in or give out. When you have come through the time of testing, turn to your companions and give them a fresh start."

Peter said, "Master, I'm ready for anything with you. I'd go to jail for you. I'd *die* for you!"

John 13:19-30, *Jesus and John*

"I'm telling you all this ahead of time so that when it happens you will believe that I am who I say I am. Make sure you get this right: Receiving someone I send is the same as receiving me, just as receiving me is the same as receiving the One who sent me."

After he said these things, Jesus became visibly upset, and then he told them why. "One of you is going to betray me."

The disciples looked around at one another, wondering who on earth he was talking about. One of the disciples, the one Jesus loved dearly, was reclining against him, his head on his shoulder. Peter motioned to him to ask who Jesus might be talking about. So, being the closest, he said, "Master, who?"

Jesus said, "The one to whom I give this crust of bread after I've dipped it." Then he dipped the crust and gave it to Judas, son of Simon the Iscariot. As soon as the bread was in his hand, Satan entered him.

"What you must do," said Jesus, "do. Do it and get it over with."

No one around the supper table knew why he said this to him. Some thought that since Judas was their treasurer, Jesus was telling him to buy what they needed for the Feast, or that he should give something to the poor.

Judas, with the piece of bread, left. It was night.

Luke 10:38-41, *Jesus, Mary, and Martha*

> As they continued their travel, Jesus entered a village. A
> woman by the name of Martha welcomed him and made
> him feel quite at home. She had a sister, Mary, who sat
> before the Master, hanging on every word he said. But
> Martha was pulled away by all she had to do in the kitchen.
> Later, she stepped in, interrupting them. "Master, don't you
> care that my sister has abandoned the kitchen to me? Tell
> her to lend me a hand."
>
> The Master said, "Martha, dear Martha, you're fussing
> far too much and getting yourself worked up over nothing.
> One thing only is essential, and Mary has chosen it — it's
> the main course, and won't be taken from her."

John 11:1-44, *Jesus and Lazarus*

> A man was sick, Lazarus of Bethany, the town of Mary and
> her sister Martha. This was the same Mary who massaged
> the Lord's feet with aromatic oils and then wiped them
> with her hair. It was her brother Lazarus who was sick. So
> the sisters sent word to Jesus, "Master, the one you love so
> very much is sick."

When Jesus got the message, he said, "This sickness is not fatal. It will become an occasion to show God's glory by glorifying God's Son."

Jesus loved Martha and her sister and Lazarus, but oddly, when he heard that Lazarus was sick, he stayed on where he was for two more days. After the two days, he said to his disciples, "Let's go back to Judea."

They said, "Rabbi, you can't do that. The Jews are out to kill you, and you're going back?"

Jesus replied, "Are there not twelve hours of daylight? Anyone who walks in daylight doesn't stumble because there's plenty of light from the sun. Walking at night, he might very well stumble because he can't see where he's going."

He said these things, and then announced, "Our friend Lazarus has fallen asleep. I'm going to wake him up."

The disciples said, "Master, if he's gone to sleep, he'll get a good rest and wake up feeling fine." Jesus was talking about death, while his disciples thought he was talking about taking a nap.

Then Jesus became explicit: "Lazarus died. And I am glad for your sakes that I wasn't there. You're about to be given new grounds for believing. Now let's go to him."

That's when Thomas, the one called the Twin, said to his companions, "Come along. We might as well die with him."

When Jesus finally got there, he found Lazarus already four days dead. Bethany was near Jerusalem, only a couple of miles away, and many of the Jews were visiting Martha and Mary, sympathizing with them over their brother. Martha heard Jesus was coming and went out to meet him. Mary remained in the house.

Martha said, "Master, if you'd been here, my brother wouldn't have died. Even now, I know that whatever you ask God he will give you."

Jesus said, "Your brother will be raised up."

Martha replied, "I know that he will be raised up in the resurrection at the end of time."

"You don't have to wait for the End. I am, right now, Resurrection and Life. The one who believes in me, even though he or she dies, will live. And everyone who lives believing in me does not ultimately die at all. Do you believe this?"

"Yes, Master. All along I have believed that you are the

Messiah, the Son of God who comes into the world."

After saying this, she went to her sister Mary and whispered in her ear, "The Teacher is here and is asking for you."

The moment she heard that, she jumped up and ran out to him. Jesus had not yet entered the town but was still at the place where Martha had met him. When her sympathizing Jewish friends saw Mary run off, they followed her, thinking she was on her way to the tomb to weep there. Mary came to where Jesus was waiting and fell at his feet, saying, "Master, if only you had been here, my brother would not have died."

When Jesus saw her sobbing and the Jews with her sobbing, a deep anger welled up within him. He said, "Where did you put him?"

"Master, come and see," they said. Now Jesus wept. The Jews said, "Look how deeply he loved him."

Others among them said, "Well, if he loved him so much, why didn't he do something to keep him from dying? After all, he opened the eyes of a blind man."

Then Jesus, the anger again welling up within him, arrived at the tomb. It was a simple cave in the hillside with a slab of stone laid against it. Jesus said, "Remove the stone."

The sister of the dead man, Martha, said, "Master, by this time there's a stench. He's been dead four days!"

Jesus looked her in the eye. "Didn't I tell you that if you believed, you would see the glory of God?"

Then, to the others, "Go ahead, take away the stone."

They removed the stone. Jesus raised his eyes to heaven and prayed, "Father, I'm grateful that you have listened to me. I know you always do listen, but on account of this crowd standing here I've spoken so that they might believe that you sent me."

Then he shouted, "Lazarus, come out!" And he came out, a cadaver, wrapped from head to toe, and with a kerchief over his face.

Jesus told them, "Unwrap him and let him loose."

Mark 3:20-21, *Jesus and the disciples*

Jesus came home and, as usual, a crowd gathered — so many making demands on him that there wasn't even time to eat. His friends heard what was going on and went to rescue him, by force if necessary. They suspected he was getting carried away with himself.

John 13:1-17, *Jesus and Peter*

Just before the Passover Feast, Jesus knew that the time had
come to leave this world to go to the Father. Having loved
his dear companions, he continued to love them right to the
end. It was suppertime. The Devil by now had Judas, son of
Simon the Iscariot, firmly in his grip, all set for the betrayal.

Jesus knew that the Father had put him in complete
charge of everything, that he came from God and was on
his way back to God. So he got up from the supper table, set
aside his robe, and put on an apron. Then he poured water
into a basin and began to wash the feet of the disciples,
drying them with his apron. When he got to Simon Peter,
Peter said, "Master, *you* wash *my* feet?"

Jesus answered, "You don't understand now what I'm
doing, but it will be clear enough to you later."

Peter persisted, "You're not going to wash my feet — ever!"

Jesus said, "If I don't wash you, you can't be part of
what I'm doing."

"Master!" said Peter. "Not only my feet, then. Wash my
hands! Wash my head!"

Jesus said, "If you've had a bath in the morning, you
only need your feet washed now and you're clean from

head to toe. My concern, you understand, is holiness, not
hygiene. So now you're clean. But not every one of you."
(He knew who was betraying him. That's why he said, "Not
every one of you.") After he had finished washing their feet,
he took his robe, put it back on, and went back to his place
at the table.

Then he said, "Do you understand what I have done to
you? You address me as 'Teacher' and 'Master,' and rightly
so. That is what I am. So if I, the Master and Teacher,
washed your feet, you must now wash each other's feet.
I've laid down a pattern for you. What I've done, you do.
I'm only pointing out the obvious. A servant is not ranked
above his master; an employee doesn't give orders to the
employer. If you understand what I'm telling you, act like
it — and live a blessed life.

John 20:11-18, *Jesus and Mary*

But Mary stood outside the tomb weeping. As she wept,
she knelt to look into the tomb and saw two angels sitting
there, dressed in white, one at the head, the other at the
foot of where Jesus' body had been laid. They said to her,
"Woman, why do you weep?"

"They took my Master," she said, "and I don't know where they put him." After she said this, she turned away and saw Jesus standing there. But she didn't recognize him.

Jesus spoke to her, "Woman, why do you weep? Who are you looking for?"

She, thinking that he was the gardener, said, "Mister, if you took him, tell me where you put him so I can care for him."

Jesus said, "Mary."

Turning to face him, she said in Hebrew, "*Rabboni*!" meaning "Teacher!"

Jesus said, "Don't cling to me, for I have not yet ascended to the Father. Go to my brothers and tell them, 'I ascend to my Father and your Father, my God and your God.'"

Mary Magdalene went, telling the news to the disciples: "I saw the Master!" And she told them everything he said to her.

"Don't be afraid, friend. Peace.
Everything is going to be all right.
Take courage. Be strong."

—DANIEL 10:19

So, my dear Christian friends,
companions in following this call to the heights,
take a good hard look at Jesus.
He's the centerpiece of everything we believe.

—HEBREWS 3:1

*My dear friends, don't let public opinion
influence how you live out our
glorious, Christ-originated faith.*

—JAMES 2:1

Don't overlook the obvious here, friends.
With God, one day is as good as
a thousand years, a thousand years as a day.

—2 PETER 3:8

But you, dear friends, carefully build yourselves up
in this most holy faith by praying in the Holy Spirit,
staying right at the center of God's love,
keeping your arms open and outstretched,
ready for the mercy of our Master, Jesus Christ.
This is the unending life, the real life!

—JUDE 20-21

Friend, don't go along with evil.
Model the good. The person who does good does God's work.
The person who does evil falsifies God,
doesn't know the first thing about God.

—3 JOHN 11